MERCENARIES IN THE VIETNAM WAR

Washington's Hiring of South Korean Soldiers

Charles M. Hernández

DEDICATION

To my fiancée, Melis, who is not only incredibly smart,
but also full of kindness in her heart;
thank you for always encouraging me to do my best.

CONTENTS

LIST OF ACRONYMS AND ABBREVIATIONS

DM	Deutsche Marks
EPB	Economic Planning Board
FYP	Five-Year Plan
G20	Group of Twenty
GVN	South Vietnamese Government
KMOD	Korean Ministry of Defense
MACV	Military Assistance Command, Vietnam
NKPA	North Korean People's Army
NVA	North Vietnamese Army
PX	Postal Exchange
ROK	Republic of Korea
ROKF-V	Republic of Korea Forces, Vietnam
SEATO	Southeast Asia Treaty Organization
SVN	South Vietnam
US	United States
USFK	United States Forces Korea
USSR	Union of Soviet Socialist Republics
VC	Viet Cong
ROK-MAG-V	Republic of Korea Military Assistance Group Vietnam

MERCENARIES IN THE VIETNAM WAR

PREFACE

***

ARGUMENT

Mercenaries in the Vietnam War explores the American efforts during the Vietnam War to recruit third-world countries with a strong emphasis on the Republic of Korea (ROK). It seeks to investigate the reasons behind South Korea's involvement in the Vietnam War. This analysis will focus on three factors: 1) America's military involvement in the Korean Peninsula. 2) Korean President Park Chung Hee and his model for economic development. 3) Legacy of the Vietnam War on the Korean economy.

Conventional wisdom of the conflict suggests that the ROK operated its military forces freely and independently without substantial American help in assisting its Far Eastern neighbor.[1] This viewpoint, however, will be challenged by examining four factors illustrating that the ROK's army operated as a mercenary force hired by the United States: 1) President Lyndon B. Johnson's "More Flags" program. 2) Detailing why other Allied forces participating in the war are not classified as mercenaries. 3) Washington's complete financial support of the ROK's involvement in Vietnam. 4) The verbal agreement established by US-ROK commanders regarding operational control of South Korean military forces.

---

[1] Larsen, Stanley R., and James Lawton Collins, *Allied Participation in Vietnam*, (Washington: Dept. of the Army: U.S. Govt). 1975. p.134

3

Through an examination of all factors, the reader will conclude that a synthesis of Park Chung Hee's resilience to spur Korean economic growth by acquiring foreign funding and establishing the legitimacy of his authoritarian rule. As well as a blank check of American financial assistance for South Korean forces in Vietnam, and secret agreements made with the US over operational control were the most compelling factors to classify the ROK's army as a mercenary force in service to America.

SCOPE

The scope of *Mercenaries in the Vietnam War* is necessarily limited to the recruitment and involvement of South Korean military forces in the Vietnam War. Although there is ample evidence of joint ROK-US-GVN operations in the final stages of the conflict, this literary work will only illustrate clashes between the NVA/VC and ROK where South Korean troops operated as a sole unit under direct American orders.

The book will investigate how South Korean troops became classified as mercenaries rather than provide anecdotal descriptions of every skirmish involving the ROK in the nearly decade long conflict. Not only would such descriptions obfuscate the core argument of the author, but also the frequencies and distinctions of the parties participating in such clashes are extremely complex and difficult to differentiate.

STRUCTURE

Mercenaries in the Vietnam War is categorized into four sections. First, it will define the term "mercenary" and illustrate the required guidelines to classify one as a professional soldier set by the Geneva Convention. Second, it will analyze the three factors illustrating America's relationship with Korea and Park Chung Hee's authoritarian government. Third, it will analyze the four factors detailing why the South Korean soldiers sent to Vietnam were considered a mercenary force. Finally, it will briefly touch on the consequences of the ROK's involvement in the conflict and its worldwide implications.

INTRODUCTION

Historical Context and Overview of the Vietnam War

***

(The national flags of the Republic of Korea, Republic of Vietnam, and the United States flying at Da Nang Air Base, 1968) [2]

---

[2] Edward Marek, "Talking Proud," *Capital "Tiger" Division*. Web. (4 Dec. 2013).
<http://www.talkingproud.us/Military/ROKVIetnam/ROKVIetnamTiger/ROKVIetnamTiger.html>.

Vietnam was the most unpopular American war of the 20th century and until recently America's longest conflict. It resulted in the death of 58, 209 US soldiers and the involvement of over 2.5 million Americans serving their country.[3] The Vietnam War has remained a bitter memory for veterans and citizens around the world. Many often ask whether the American effort in South Vietnam (SVN) was a senseless blunder creating an unnecessary war, or an idealistic attempt with a noble cause to protect the Vietnamese population from the grip of Communism.

In 1954, the Vietnamese successfully defeated the French at the battle of Dien Bien Phu after a decade long anti-colonial war.[4] At the peace conference in Geneva, Vietnam received its independence and the country was temporarily divided at the 17th parallel with an anti-communist government to the South and a communist government to the North. By 1958, the North Vietnamese Army (NVA) and the Viet Cong (VC), a communist-led guerilla, sought to unify the entire nation and began to battle the South Vietnamese government.[5]

Through this timeframe, the US gradually increased its military presence in Vietnam. Following the Gulf of Tonkin incident in 1964, US President Lyndon B. Johnson escalated the war by commencing air strikes and committing combat forces to the country, which led to a peak presence of 536,000 American soldiers in 1968.[6] That same year,

---

[3] *Vietnam in HD*. Dir. Michael Hall. Perf. Adrian Grenier . A & E Home Video, 2011. Blu-Ray.
[4] "Digital History," *Digital History*. (1 Dec 2013).
<http://www.digitalhistory.uh.edu/era.cfm?eraid=18&smtid=1>.
[5] Ibid. 2925
[6] "Digital History," *Digital History*. (1 Dec 2013).
<http://www.digitalhistory.uh.edu/era.cfm?eraid=18&smtid=1>.

however, the North Vietnamese launched the Tet Offensive, which resulted in a psychological victory for the communists. It severely weakened US morale and shattered America's expectations of a quick victory.

The following president, Richard Nixon, advocated Vietnamization, the complete withdrawal of American troops, and assigning the South Vietnamese government (GVN) with greater responsibility for fighting the war.[7] In 1970, Nixon sent ground forces into Cambodia to slow the supply of NVA troops and weaponry into South Vietnam. This action was met with massive anti-war movements protesting the increasingly unpopular and endless war. In 1973, all fighting political parties reached a diplomatic agreement; US forces were withdrawn and American prisoners of war were released. Two years later, however, the GVN surrendered to the NVA, and Vietnam was unified under the banner of Communism.[8]

---

[7] Ibid. 3468
[8] Ibid. 3464

Why Vietnam? American Goals

US involvement in Vietnam was determined by three major factors:

1. Cold War fears led the US to overestimate the geopolitical importance of Vietnam: The Kennedy and Johnson Administration believed the fall of the country would lead to communist domination of Indochina. Both administrations held a mistaken belief that North Vietnam was a pawn of Moscow.[9]

2. World events occurring at the time impacted the Western perception of communism's influence: "The erection of the Berlin Wall, the Bay of Pigs incident, and the threat made by Soviet Premier Nikita Khrushchev to sponsor national liberation movements around the world."[10] The US would have to implement a policy of containment to stop the spread of communism.

3. Domestic politics at the home front contributed to American involvement in the war: US Presidents John F. Kennedy and Lyndon B. Johnson feared that failure to achieve victory in South Vietnam would hinder their chances for "…re-election, weaken support for domestic social programs, and make Democrats vulnerable to the charge of being soft on communism."[11]

One of the fascinating aspects of the Vietnam War is that the

---

[9] Ibid. 3462
[10] Digital History," *Digital History*. (1 Dec 2013). <http://www.digitalhistory.uh.edu/era.cfm?eraid=18&smtid=1
[11] Ibid. 3462

military mission of the United States (US) changed multiple times during the conflict even though its grand strategy of containment remained in place. Tactically, for the first time in American history, success in the battlefield was to be measured through body count and not territorial control. Eventually, the US attempted to bomb the North into submission, and finally, the American counter-insurgency strategy sought to achieve victory by winning the hearts and minds of the South Vietnamese people. None of these military strategies impeded the spread of communism throughout SVN.

Map of Vietnam

<u>Timeline of War</u>: [12]

[12] "Primary source: "Myth vs. Reality" by B.G. Burkett and GlennaWhitley," *Vietnam (RVN) War Chronology/Timeline*. (7 December 2013) <http://cybersarges.tripod.com/timeline.html>.

1. WHAT IS A MERCENARY?

***

Defining the Profession

From the Battle of Kadesh to the sands of Syria, mercenaries have played an active role in the reported history of war. The term originates from the Latin root "merces" or wages.[13] Contemporary dictionaries define a mercenary as a person who serves merely for wages or a soldier hired into foreign service.[14] Article 47 of Additional Protocol I within the Geneva Conventions sets six strict conditions that must all be met for a person to be considered a mercenary:

"A) Is specially recruited locally or abroad in order to fight in an armed conflict;

B) Does, in fact, take a direct part in the hostilities;

C) Is motivated to take part in the hostilities essentially by the desire for private gain and, in fact, is promised, by or on behalf of a Party to the conflict, material compensation substantially in excess of that promised or paid to combatants of similar ranks and functions in the armed forces of that Party;

D) Is neither a national of a Party to the conflict nor a resident of territory controlled by a Party to the conflict;

E) Is not a member of the armed forces of a Party to the conflict; and

F) Has not been sent by a State which is not a Party to the conflict on official duty as a member of its armed forces."[15]

---

[13] "Mercenary," *Merriam-Webster*. Merriam-Webster. (8 December 2013). <http://www.merriam-webster.com/dictionary/mercenary>.

[14] *Shadow company*. Dir. Nick Bicanic . Perf. Alan Bell, Phil Lancaster. Purpose Built Film, 2006.

[15] "Customary IHL - Rule 108. Mercenaries," *Customary IHL - Rule 108. Mercenaries*. (6 December 2013). <http://www.icrc.org/customary-ihl/eng/docs/v1_rul_rule108>.

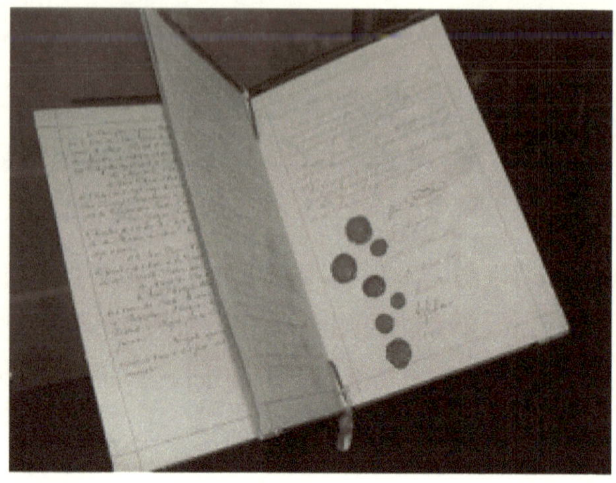

The original document of the first Geneva Convention (1864). [16]

There has always been a negative connotation attached to the word mercenary. In *Just and Unjust Wars*, Michael Walzer states that society's ordinary depiction of a mercenary is construed as a brutal individual who rapes, pillages, and tortures the people of areas under his occupation.[17] However, soldiers throughout history have committed identical crimes and they were not classified as mercenaries. It is important to distinguish the fundamental difference between an ordinary soldier and a mercenary. In *Shadow Company*, Dr. Eike Kluge asserts that a soldier fights under a flag for a particular country that has a legitimate use of force, which allows him to engage in activities that would otherwise be considered criminal or murderous. A mercenary, on the other hand, lacks this immediate social justification for he fights and earns pay from a foreign government in a cause that is not of his

---

[16] "Geneva Conventions," *Wikipedia*. (8 December 2013).
<http://en.wikipedia.org/wiki/File:Original_Geneva_Conventions.jpg>
[17] Walzer, Michael, *Just and unjust wars: a moral argument with historical illustrations*. 4th ed. New York: Basic Books,1977. p. 27

country.[18] As a result, society holds a hereditary recollection of negativity toward the mercenary profession.

18 *Shadow company*. Dir. Nick Bicanic . Perf. Alan Bell, Phil Lancaster. Purpose Built Film, 2006.

2. ANALYSIS OF THE FACTORS BEHIND THE REPUBLIC OF KOREA'S INVOLVEMENT IN THE VIETNAM WAR

Modern Day Korea and its Humble Origins

The world of the 21st century is overflowing with wealth, but some scenes contradict this abundance. Korea was once a country in abject poverty with its natural resources depleted through the Japanese occupation and its land ravaged by war. Upon reviewing the nation in 1953, US General Douglas MacArthur stated, "This country has no future. This country will not be restored even after a hundred years."[19] However, Korea in less than sixty years has managed to become a global power with an amazingly rapid and successful technological transformation.

The nation currently ranks as the 12th largest economy in the world becoming the first Asian nation to host the Group of Twenty (G20) Seoul Summit in 2010.[20] Additionally, Korea has become a premier-class manufacturing country comprising the world's largest shipbuilding industry and fifth-largest automobile, steel, and crude oil distillation industries.[21]

How did Korea manage to escape the clutches of poverty and achieve such astounding success? To answer this question, one must look at the nation's modern history, specifically, Korea's relationship with the United States during the Cold War period.

---

[19] "Secrets behind Korea's Economic Success." *YouTube*. The Korea Foundation. (5 May 2014). <https://www.youtube.com/watch?v=bJ0hMr5TSkI>.

[20] Ibid.

[21] "Park Chung-Hee and the Economy of South Korea." N.p., n.d: p. 1.

Contemporary History of Korea

<u>1) The Cold War: America's Military Involvement in the Korean Peninsula:</u>

On August 15, 1945, Korea gained independence from the Japanese Empire. For the first time in nearly four decades, Koreans could relish their newfound freedom and liberty absent foreign oppression. However, the joy of emancipation from Japan's brutal colonial rule was swiftly dissipated with the outbreak of the Korean War.

The conflict became the first proxy war in the overarching struggle between the United States and the Union of the Soviet Socialist Republics (USSR). Although the USSR provided advisers and military resources to the conflict, no Soviet soldiers physically engaged in combat operations. Conversely, American soldiers formed a critical component of the UN coalition that reacted in response to North Korean aggression.[22]

The Korean War began on 25 June 1950, when North Korean People's Army (NKPA) forces crossed the 38th parallel with the support of a massive artillery barrage and Russian advisers without warning.[23] This strategy was known as the Great Naktong Offensive. The U.N. responded with a call to arms, and a coalition of nations including the Republic of Korea (ROK), the United States, Britain, Australia, and

---

[22] Kyle Gaines, *The Decisive Factors in the UN Forces' Defense of the Pusan Perimeter in the 1950 Korean War,* (Potomac Foundation). p. 2

[23] Harry G Summers, Jr., *Korean War Almanac,* (New York, NY: Facts on File Inc., 1990). p. xiii

Turkey committed troops and resources to the defense of South Korea.[24] NKPA forces advanced rapidly throughout the country taking the South Korean capital, Seoul, within days. By early August, North Korea controlled all territory in South Korea except a southeastern portion of the peninsula known as Pusan.

The UN commitment of troops and American efforts to stem the North Korean advance led to the hasty creation of a defensive perimeter along Pusan under US Eighth Army General Walton Walker[25] (See Figure 4). Although heavily outnumbered, the war was changing character. The American and South Korean force was no longer relying on ineffective weapons and a lack of armor to stem the tide of a relatively well-organized and equipped enemy.[26] Miraculously, the UN force was able to hold the NKPA at the Pusan Perimeter, which bought time for Gen. Douglas MacArthur's famous Inchon invasion on September 15, 1950.[27]

After the invasion at Inchon, UN forces successfully pushed back NKPA forces to the 38th parallel and then pressed their advance up the peninsula towards the Yalu River.[28] At this stage in the war, however, Chinese Communist Forces (CCF) entered the fray and from December 1950 to June 1951, launched a daunting offensive that drove UN forces back down to the 38th parallel.[29] From July 1951 until the armistice in July 1953, the Korean War resembled the static trench

---

[24] Harry G Summers, Jr., *Korean War Almanac*, (New York, NY: Facts on File Inc., 1990). p. xiv
[25] Edwin P. Hoyt, *The Pusan Perimeter, Korea, 1950*, (Briarcliff Manor, NY: Stein and Day Publishers, 1984). p. 139
[26] Ibid. 139
[27] Ibid. xiv
[28] Ibid.
[29] Ibid.

warfare that engulfed World War I and ultimately concluded with a ceasefire between North and South Korea.[30]

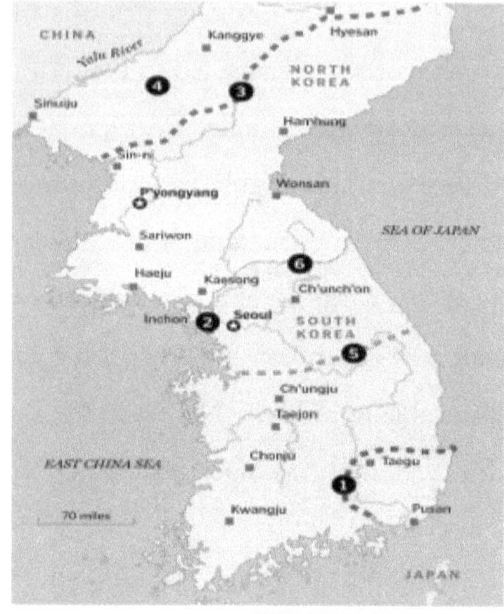

Figure 4. [31]

***

---

[30] Kyle Gaines, *The Decisive Factors in the UN Forces' Defense of the Pusan Perimeter in the 1950 Korean War,* (Potomac Foundation). p. 3

[31] J. McCracken, "A Brief Timeline of the Korean War" (15 November 2012). <http://jmccrackenworld.com/KoreanWarBrief.jpg>

Aftermath of the Korean War

The Korean War was utterly devastating for the newly independent nation of South Korea. Hope and the expectation of building a prosperous unified nation disappeared in the fog of fratricidal war.[32] Unprepared and unable to recover from the ruins of war on its own, the Syngman Rhee government relied heavily on American foreign aid. The nation's budget soon consisted of over 90% of Western donations.[33]

For over ten years, the Rhee government failed to create any economic growth in South Korea.[34] The country became the poorest of 120 nations in the United Nations with an income per capita of less than $67.[35] Absolute and inescapable poverty was an ever-present reality as thousands of Korean peasants reportedly starved to death on the streets of the capital, Seoul.[36]

At this time, North Korea surpassed the South in every aspect of its economy. The Communist threat was at its highest with Northern military build-up along the border and isolated confrontations increasing per year. Another war between the Korean people appeared inevitable. Domestic fears of a Northern invasion quickly spread throughout the country.

---

[32] Park, Chung Hee. *Korea Reborn: A Model for Development*. Englewood Cliffs, N.J.: Prentice-Hall, 1979. p. 13.

[33] "Secrets behind Korea's Economic Success." *YouTube*. The Korea Foundation. (5 May 2014). <https://www.youtube.com/watch?v=bJ0hMr5TSkI>.

[34] "Park Chung-Hee and the Economy of South Korea." N.p., n.d: p. 1.

[35] Ibid.

*Amount converted to 2014 USD – Inflation calculated.

[36] Ibid.

1) Park Chung Hee – The Miracle Worker of the Han River:

Under the midst of darkness in 1961, Major General Park Chung Hee led a military coup d'état composed of 3,000 Korean soldiers in what became known as the May 16th Revolution. General Park felt that most of the problems Koreans faced after the War were caused by the sheer incompetence and corruption of the Rhee Government and its monopoly control over political power.[37] He established a Bureaucratic Authoritarian Regime centering economic development and strengthening of domestic defense as the nation's top priorities.[38]

General Park took office with an achievement-oriented approach promoting military-style discipline and efficiency. He was convinced that bureaucratic autonomy was the most effective means of achieving national reconstruction and the consolidation of his political leadership.

The Korean president concentrated all social, political, and economic power under his command. However, he still faced two enormous obstacles: The acquisition of monetary funds for economic development programs and the potential withdrawal of American military forces from the Korean Peninsula.

---

[37] Kim, Hyung. *Korea's development under Park Chung Hee rapid industrialization, 1961-79.* London: RoutledgeCurzon, 2004. p. 41.

[38] "Park Chung-Hee and the Economy of South Korea." N.p., n.d: p. 3.

[Maj. Gen. Park Chung Hee (front right) overviewing the May 19 Coup].[39]

[39] "May 16 coup." *Wikipedia*. Wikimedia Foundation, 5 Aug. 2014. Web. 8 May 2014.
<http://en.wikipedia.org/wiki/May_16_coup>.

The Challenges

President Park intended to transform Korea from an agrarian society to an urban and industrial nation. In 1961, he established the Economic Planning Board (EPB) with the sole responsibility of creating a Five-Year Plan (FYP) blueprint for economic development.[40] The EPB was granted unprecedented powers in planning, allocating the national budget, and attracting foreign investment. The programs of the FYP were organized in four phases beginning in 1962.

Year	Five Year Plan
1962-1966	The goal was to build a self-reliant industrial structure.
1967-1971	The goal was to modernize the industrial structure and to build import substitution industries.
1972-1976	The goal was to build an export-oriented industrial structure by promoting heavy and chemical industries.
1977-1981	The goal was to promote development of industries that can effectively compete internationally in industrial export markets.

(FYP of South Korea During the Era of Park Chung Hee).[41]

In order to carry out each phase, the Park regime required substantial financial capital. Unfortunately, Korea was in the midst of economic bankruptcy. President Park knew the greatest challenge for his regime would be the acquisition of funds. He initially addressed the problem through diplomatic contracts. Park dispatched a temporary workforce of miners and nurses to West Germany in return for 140 million Deutsche Marks (DM). Additionally, these Korean citizens were forced to send their earnings back home so that the Park regime could

---

[40] "Park Chung-Hee and the Economy of South Korea." N.p., n.d: p. 4.
[41] Ibid.

utilize their checks as collateral for German loans.[42] President Park then pursued a quick settlement with Japan in terms of reparation funds and diplomatic normalization.[43] The settlement provided Korea with $800 million in grants and preferential loans as compensation for Japanese colonial wrongdoing.[44] The final obstacle for the Park regime was to attain American political and financial support of Korea's FYP.

In 1961, American monetary aid constituted a lifeline for South Korea. The US supplied over 73 percent of the country's annual imports and shared about 12 percent of its gross national product.[45] President Park viewed the US as a necessary resource for Korea's economic development and national security.[46] However, Park's rule coincided with a sharp decline in annual US economic aid from $230 million to $110 million.[47] Furthermore, Cold War policies were increasingly shifting the US military toward Indochina. The president personally interpreted this decline as a withdrawal of US commitment from South Korea. Within his inner circle, there was a deeply ingrained fear of American abandonment.

---

[42] "Secrets behind Korea's Economic Success." *YouTube*. The Korea Foundation. (5 May 2014). <https://www.youtube.com/watch?v=bJ0hMr5TSkI>.

[43] Won-soon, Park. "Korea-Japan Treaty, Breakthrough for Nation Building." *The Korea Times*. N.p., 19 Mar. 2010. (5 May 2014). <http://www.koreatimes.co.kr/www/news/biz/2013/11/291_62653.html>.

[44] Lee, Min Y. "The Vietnam War: South Korea's Search for National Security." *International Relations*. 403-29. (18 Apr. 2012). p. 426. <https://campus.georgetown.edu/bbcswebdav/pid-2443148-dt-content-rid-2105902_1/courses/HIST-226-01.Spring2012/DOC001-4%281%29.PDF>.

[45] Ibid. 407

[46] Kim, Hyung. *Korea's development under Park Chung Hee rapid industrialization, 1961-79*. London: RoutledgeCurzon, 2004. p. 93.

[47] Ibid. 407

Alluring the Americans

In the aftermath of the May 16th Revolution, the US was initially apprehensive to formally recognize Park Chung Hee as the legitimate president of South Korea. However, Park knew that American acquiescence was needed to sustain his authoritarian rule.[48] During his first visit to Washington in November 1961, President Park informed US President Kennedy, that South Korea was ready to dispatch troops to Vietnam if requested to contribute with the security of the Far East from Communism. President Kennedy expressed deep appreciation, noting that the US was carrying "…the burden from Berlin all the way around the globe."[49]

(President Park meets President John F. Kennedy and his wife in 1961).[50]

---

[48] Ibid. 406

[49] *Foreign Relations of the United States, 1961-1963* XXII (1961). p. 2.

[50] "Meeting with General Chung Hee Park, Chairman, Supreme Council of Korea, 3:30PM." - *John F. Kennedy Presidential Library & Museum*. N.p., n.d. (8 May 2014).
<http://www.jfklibrary.org/Asset-Viewer/Archives/JFKWHP-1961-11-14-C.aspx>.
*At the time of this picture, the JFK Administration had not formally recognized Park Chung Hee as

Park argued that such action would prove that there was unity among the nations of the Free World. However, the Korean president held ulterior motives. The potential deployment of Korean troops to Vietnam was aimed not only to secure US approval of his regime but also to maximize the economic and security opportunities to be gained by supporting American led Cold War policy in East Asia.[51]

A year later, Park received an official request from the Ngo Dinh Diem government for South Korean military assistance. The US followed with a formal request for South Korean forces on May 1, 1964, with President Johnson's escalation of the conflict.[52] Nevertheless, the Johnson Administration toyed with Park's fear of American abandonment. To completely secure Korean involvement in Vietnam, US ambassador Winthrop Brown hinted that "USFK troops might have to be withdrawn if Park decided not to dispatch combat troops to South Vietnam."[53] Upon hearing this news, Korean foreign minister Yi Tongwôn recommended that Park focus primarily on the economic side-payments if the dispatch of troops to Vietnam was inevitable.[54] From then on, Park negotiated the dispatch and expansion of Korean forces at a calculated and profitable price.

Korea's president. Hence, the military title associated with his name during the visit.

[51] Kim, Hyung. *Korea's development under Park Chung Hee rapid industrialization, 1961-79.* London: RoutledgeCurzon, 2004. p. 102.

[52] Lee, Min Y. "The Vietnam War: South Korea's Search for National Security." *International Relations.* 403-29. (18 Apr. 2012). p. 409. <https://campus.georgetown.edu/bbcswebdav/pid-2443148-dt-content-rid-2105902_1/courses/HIST-226-01.Spring2012/DOC001-4%281%29.PDF>.

[53] Ibid. 410

[54] Ibid. 412

1) Legacy of the Vietnam War on the Korean Economy

ROK participation in Vietnam was only made possible through American willingness to subsidize all Korean civil-military operations in-country; a commitment outlined and signed by Seoul and Washington in the Brown Memorandum.[55] From 1964 to 1965, revenues from the Vietnam War totaled 40% of Korea's foreign exchange earnings, and from 1965 to 1972, the country earned an estimated $1 billion in hard US currency and received $2.7 billion in foreign loans.[56] Additionally, the Nixon Administration appropriated $1.5 billion to South Korea's Five-Year Military Modernization Plan (1971-1975).[57] The dispatch of Korean troops as well secured an export market for South Korean goods and services across Vietnam.[58] In all, the Park regime earned approximately $5 billion during eight years of ROK deployments to Vietnam.[59]

While scholars have yet to present a detailed correlation between the Vietnam War and Korea's economic growth, it is reasonable to conclude that ROK participation in the conflict contributed to the nation's rapid economic development. During the timeframe of ROK

---

[55] "U.S. paid S.Korean victims of Vietnam War." *UPI*. N.p. (5 May 2014).
<http://www.upi.com/Top_News/2005/12/02/US-paid-SKorean-victims-of-Vietnam-War/UPI-80431133524267/>.
[56] Lee, Min Y. "The Vietnam War: South Korea's Search for National Security." *International Relations*. 403-29. (18 Apr. 2012). p. 426.
<https://campus.georgetown.edu/bbcswebdav/pid-2443148-dt-content-rid-2105902_1/courses/HIST-226-01.Spring2012/DOC001-4%281%29.PDF>.
[57] Ibid. 423
[58] Ibid. 408
[59] Baek, Glen. "A Perspective on Korea's Participation in the Vietnam War." *The Asan Institute for Policy Studies* 53 (2013). p. 4.

deployments, Korea's GDP increased four-fold. It is estimated that the financial gains from the Vietnam War accounted for 7-8 percent of Korea's GDP from 1966 to 1969.[60] President Park utilized the influx of capital to spur his ambitious FYD programs. As a result, the conflict coincided with Park's export-oriented industrialization program (1967-1972), which sought to establish conglomerates known as Chaebols through subsidized loans, price controls, and tax reductions. The EPB protected these newly formed domestic markets by implementing high import quotas.[61]

---

[60] Ibid. 4
*Korea's GDP was US$2.7 billion in 1963 and US$10.73 billion in 1973.
[61] "Park Chung-Hee and the Economy of South Korea." N.p., n.d: p. 7.

Park Chung Hee's Invisible Hand

The Vietnam War proved to be a lucrative economic and political venture for Park Chung Hee. Korea's contribution to the war enabled the Park regime to secure the necessary capital to jump-start its ambitious economic development plans of the late 1960s and early 1970s. American support of Park's authoritarian government allowed the Korean president to quell all domestic opposition without the worry of international reprisal.[62] Finally, the Korean government took full advantage of US concessions to modernize its armed forces, which as of 2013 ranks eight in global military firepower.[63]

West Germany's loans, the Japanese reparation funds, and the Vietnam War had a windfall effect on the South Korean economy. In 1961, Gross Domestic Product (GDP) per capita measured $110. In 2011, the World Bank calculated Korea's GDP per capita at $20,870.[64] It's hardly a coincidence that Korea's GDP grew at a rapid pace during the years Korean troops were deployed in Vietnam. In less than four decades, the Republic of Korea, a once impoverished country referred to as a "garbage dump" by Vengalil Menon, Head of the UN Special Delegation, has transformed itself into a developed nation with the

---

[62] Lee, Min Y. "The Vietnam War: South Korea's Search for National Security." *International Relations*. 403-29. (18 Apr. 2012). p. 404.
<https://campus.georgetown.edu/bbcswebdav/pid-2443148-dt-content-rid-2105902_1/courses/HIST-226-01.Spring2012/DOC001-4%281%29.PDF>.

[63] Baek, Glen. "A Perspective on Korea's Participation in the Vietnam War." *The Asan Institute for Policy Studies* 53 (2013). p. 6.

[64] "Korea - GDP per capita." *Index Mundi*. N.p., n.d. (5 May 2014).
<http://www.indexmundi.com/facts/korea/gdp-per-capita>.

world's most advanced technological infrastructure.[65] Korea now serves as the center of export-oriented business and commerce in Asia.

---

[65] "Secrets behind Korea`s Economic Success." *YouTube*. The Korea Foundation. (5 May 2014). <https://www.youtube.com/watch?v=bJ0hMr5TSkI>.

3. ANALYSIS OF THE FACTORS DETAILING THE REPUBLIC OF KOREA AS A MERCENARY FORCE IN VIETNAM

1) The Free World Assistance Program

Today's society has often interpreted the Vietnam War as the United States fighting alone in a remote land under the banner of an imperialistic policy of containment against Communism. However, the US did not fight exclusively in the conflict. It was accompanied by a coalition of four nations that provided combat troops: the Republic of Korea, Thailand, Australia, and New Zealand.[66] Of all the Allied nations participating in the conflict, the ROK was the most involved country sending more than 300,000 troops to serve combat tours and incurring an estimated 4,407 casualties over nearly a decade.[67] The Korean Army maintained 50,000 active troops fighting side by side with US forces at the height of military intervention.[68]

American Diplomacy by the early 1960s pursued only two major goals: "the need to confront the Soviet Union and…prevent the export of its communist ideology."[69] In April 1964, US President Lyndon B. Johnson announced the "More Flags" initiative calling forth international participation to stop the spread of communism in Vietnam. It quickly became the Johnson Administration's primary instrument to obtain international consensus and assistance for America's policy in

---

[66] Colman, J. and Widen, J. J. (2009), The Johnson Administration and the Recruitment of Allies in Vietnam, 1964–1968. (2 December 2013). p. 483
<http://onlinelibrary.wiley.com/doi/10.1111/j.1468-229X.2009.00467.x/full>.

[67] Blackburn, Robert M, *Mercenaries and Lyndon Johnson's "more Flags": The Hiring of Korean, Filipino, and Thai Soldiers in the Vietnam War*. Jefferson, NC: McFarland, 1994. p. xiii

[68] Marek, Edward, "Koreans Rock-Solid in Vietnam." *Talking Proud.* (20 November 2013).
<http://www.talkingproud.us/Military/ROKVietnam/ROKVIetnamIntro.html>.

[69] Blackburn, Robert M, *Mercenaries and Lyndon Johnson's "more Flags": The Hiring of Korean, Filipino, and Thai Soldiers in the Vietnam War*. Jefferson, NC: McFarland, 1994. p. 7

South Vietnam.[70] In addition, President Johnson utilized the program to mute Congressional opposition to the war by showing widened Allied support for the conflict. [71]

More Flags initially sought only non-combat assistance. However, that original objective did not survive during its first year of existence. In March 1965, President Johnson redefined the program's purposes to "…allow for the procurement of free world troops to fight, and die, in Southeast Asia."[72] All requests for international aid to South Vietnam would now originate from Washington rather than from Saigon.[73] In essence, More Flags effectively became America's principal device through which to hire mercenary troops.

---

[70] Ibid. 13

[71] Lee, Min Y, "The Vietnam War: South Korea's Search for National Security." *International Relations*. (4 December 2013). p. 411
<https://campus.georgetown.edu/bbcswebdav/pid-2443148-dt-content-rid-2105902_1/courses/HIST-226-01.Spring2012/DOC001-4%281%29.PDF>.

[72] Ibid p.1

[73] Ibid. 16

Why did the US change the objectives of the More Flags program?

President Johnson never considered it politically expedient for the US to commit soldiers to fight alone in Indochina.[74] As the Vietnam War escalated, the US adjusted its policy and sought the assistance of foreign combat forces. US Diplomatic failure to gather support from the Southeast Asia Treaty Organization (SEATO), Western Europe's refusal to provide troops, along with increased American troop commitments, and a growing anti-war opposition gave way to President Johnson's decision to request direct military engagement from third-world nations.[75] This action required a concomitant change in the means by which the program would be prosecuted. On December 15, 1964, the Stated Department notified America's allies that the US would pay the entire cost of any free world military aid commitment to South Vietnam.[76]

---

[74] Ibid. 5

[75] Colman, J. and Widen, J. J. (2009), The Johnson Administration and the Recruitment of Allies in Vietnam, 1964–1968. (2 December 2013). p. 484 <http://onlinelibrary.wiley.com/doi/10.1111/j.1468-229X.2009.00467.x/full>.

[76] Blackburn, Robert M, *Mercenaries and Lyndon Johnson's "more Flags": The Hiring of Korean, Filipino, and Thai Soldiers in the Vietnam War*. Jefferson, NC: McFarland, 1994. p. 24

2) Allied Participation in South Vietnam and their Non Classification as Mercenaries

Much research refers to the Montagnard, an indigenous people of the Central Highlands in Vietnam, and the Meo, a group of Laotian tribesmen, as being mercenary forces.[77] However, since these people were natives to the areas of conflict, they do not fulfill the definitional requirements set by the Geneva Convention for the term mercenary. Additionally, with the exception of South Korea, all remaining Allied combat troops stationed in Vietnam are also exempt from being labeled as soldiers of fortune due to their inability to meet these strict guidelines.

In September 1966, Walt Rostow, a National Security Adviser to the US president, noted that the US did not provide any economic aid to Australia and New Zealand.[78] In fact, both countries refused to accept payment for their troops' service. Their governments even reimbursed the US for the quartering of their soldiers.[79] Rostow wrote, "Canberra and Wellington sought to strengthen their security links with the United States in an era in which British power in Asia was declining."[80] The final country, Thailand, had sound political motives for becoming military involved in the Vietnamese conflict. According to Dean Rusk, US Secretary of State, Thailand's involvement in the conflict provided the country an opportunity to modernize its armed forces and grant the

---

[77] Ibid. xiv

[78] Colman, J. and Widen, J. J. (2009), The Johnson Administration and the Recruitment of Allies in Vietnam, 1964–1968. (2 December 2013). p. 498 <http://onlinelibrary.wiley.com/doi/10.1111/j.1468-229X.2009.00467.x/full>.

[79] Blackburn, Robert M, *Mercenaries and Lyndon Johnson's "more Flags": The Hiring of Korean, Filipino, and Thai Soldiers in the Vietnam War*. Jefferson, NC: McFarland, 1994. p. 131

[80] Ibid. 499

Thai government an overall "…gambit [to] have a larger voice in determining the composition of any future peace conference and related action [in Vietnam]."[81]

ROK's Classification as a Mercenary Force

In 1954, South Korea's President Syngman Rhee proposed to aid the United States in the war against the communists by sending a military element to Vietnam.[82] President Dwight D. Eisenhower declined Rhee's request stating that "U.S. public opinion would not support the maintenance of U.S. Forces in Korea if [South] Korean forces were withdrawn from [the Korean Peninsula] for actions elsewhere."[83] This view changed dramatically a decade later when President Johnson planned to increase American forces in Vietnam to 550,000 soldiers.[84] The Administration's assessment of Korea's proposal detailed that the country "…provided the man-to-man equivalent of the Americans….In other words, every Korean soldier sent to South Vietnam saved sending an American or other allied soldier."[85] In essence, President Johnson knew that Korea's troop commitment in the war effort would temporarily minimize domestic anti-war sentiments by having to deploy fewer US soldiers. Additionally, the administration

---

[81] Ibid. 499

[82] Westmoreland, William C, *A soldier reports*. Garden City, N.Y.: Doubleday, 1976. pp. 145

[83] Lee, Min Y, "The Vietnam War: South Korea's Search for National Security." *International Relations*. (8 December 2013). p. 408
 <https://campus.georgetown.edu/bbcswebdav/pid-2443148-dt-content-rid-2105902_1/courses/HIST-226-01.Spring2012/DOC001-4%281%29.PDF>.

[84] *Vietnam in HD*, Dir. Michael Hall. Perf. Adrian Grenier . A & E Home Video, 2011. Blu-Ray.

[85] Larsen, Stanley R., and James Lawton Collins, *Allied Participation in Vietnam*, (Washington: Dept. of the Army: U.S. Govt). 1975. p. 145

acknowledged the cost-effective benefits of funding foreign troops in Vietnam. The Pentagon estimated that the cost to support a South Korean soldier's yearlong deployment was $5,000, while the cost to support an American soldier was $13,000.[86] In all, President Johnson felt that Korea's offer would benefit American interests in the US and Vietnam.

Prior to sending combatant forces to the host country in 1965, the ROK anticipated a formal request from the South Vietnamese government. This desire was due to Korean fears that the international community would view their military support as an American obligation.[87] Within weeks, the GVN officially petitioned for Korean military assistance. The Korean Ministry of Defense (KMOD) immediately responded by sending to Vietnam a "Dove Unit" composed of a Mobile Army Surgical Hospital, a construction support group, a Marine Corps engineer company, and Tae-kwon-do instructors.[88] These elements, totaling 2,416 personnel, would only remain in the country from February to June 1965. [89] They were officially designated as the Republic of Korea Military Assistance Group, Vietnam (ROK-MAG-V). The US was pleased with Korea's kind gesture of sending non-combatant assistance to Vietnam; however, the Johnson Administration began preliminary planning to hire three ROK combat divisions. ROK DOVE Unit, Figure 8. [90]

---

[86] Ibid. 416

[87] Ibid. 11

[88] Larsen, Stanley R., and James Lawton Collins, *Allied Participation in Vietnam*, (Washington: Dept. of the Army: U.S. Govt). 1975. p. 121

[89] Marek, Edward, "Koreans Rock-Solid in Vietnam." *Talking Proud.* (7 December 2013). <http://www.talkingproud.us/Military/ROKVIetnam/ROKVIetnamIntro.html>.

[90] Ibid.

***

3) Washington's Financial Support of South Korea's Presence in Vietnam

In the spring of 1965 with the introduction of American combat troops in South Vietnam, the Johnson Administration prepared to employ third world countries in the fighting as well. The US president was now more interested in the operational value of these countries rather than their prior symbolic political worth.[91]

It quickly became apparent that without American material incentives, third world countries such as the ROK would not send ground forces. The US Department of State and the Department of Defense resolved this matter by offering South Korea the following deal:

1) The Korean government would not incur any costs in the deployment of Korean divisions to Vietnam.[92]

2) The US will equip the three combat-ready Korean divisions to 100 percent.[93]

3) The US will support all logistical aspects of Korean operations in Indochina to include food, transportation, hospital supplies, etc.[94]

---

[91] Colman, J. and Widen, J. J. (2009), The Johnson Administration and the Recruitment of Allies in Vietnam, 1964–1968. (2 December 2013). p. 496 <http://onlinelibrary.wiley.com/doi/10.1111/j.1468-229X.2009.00467.x/full>.

[92] Larsen, Stanley R., and James Lawton Collins, *Allied Participation in Vietnam*, (Washington: Dept. of the Army: U.S. Govt). 1975. p. 127

[93] Ibid. 124

[94] Ibid. 131

The overall cost to the US for Korean involvement in the conflict was approximated to $2,000,000 annually, and the first year fee for the establishment of Korean divisions in Vietnam was estimated at $43,000,000.[95]

The Overall Quality of the ROK's Mercenary Force

On August 19, 1965, the Korean National Assembly, passed a bill authorizing the deployment of two Korean divisions: the Capital "Tiger" Infantry Division and the 2nd Marine Corps Brigade "Blue Dragons."[96] The final element, 9th "White Horse" Korean Division, was scheduled to dispatch a year later. These divisions held the longest service records during the Korean War and significant prestige in the country. [97]

South Korean president Park Chung-hee insisted that only volunteers be sent to Vietnam. To attract prospective enlistments, the government offered inducements for soldiers to join the divisions: "[Each recruit] would receive credit for three years of military duty for each year served in Vietnam as well as additional monetary entitlements."[98]

These incentives provided the ROK with a large applicant pool. The Korean Army set up a screening process for selection basing it on Soldiers' combat experience, motivation, and discipline. Commanders

---

[95] Ibid. 127
[96] Ibid. 128
[97] Ibid. 145
[98] Larsen, Stanley R., and James Lawton Collins, *Allied Participation in Vietnam*, (Washington: Dept. of the Army: U.S. Govt). 1975. p. 143

were able to handpick the most outstanding applicants who they wished to accompany their units in Vietnam. [99]

Time Dispatched	Organization	Strength
1964- 1965	Medical and engineer groups (Dove)	2,128
1965	Capital Division (-RCT) with support forces and Marine brigade	18,904
1966	9th Division with RCT and support forces	23,865
1967	Marine battalion (-) and other support forces	2,963
1969	C-46 crews, authorized increase	12

(ROK volunteers assigned to Vietnam). [100] [101]

---

[99] Ibid. 141

[100] Marek, Edward, "Koreans Rock-Solid in Vietnam." *Talking Proud.* (8 May 2014). <http://www.talkingproud.us/Military/ROKVIetnam/ROKVIetnamIntro.html>.

[101] Marek, Edward, "Koreans Rock-Solid in Vietnam." *Talking Proud.* (8 May 2014). <http://www.talkingproud.us/Military/ROKVIetnam/ROKVIetnamIntro.html>.

South Korean Military Forces – Area of Operations [102]

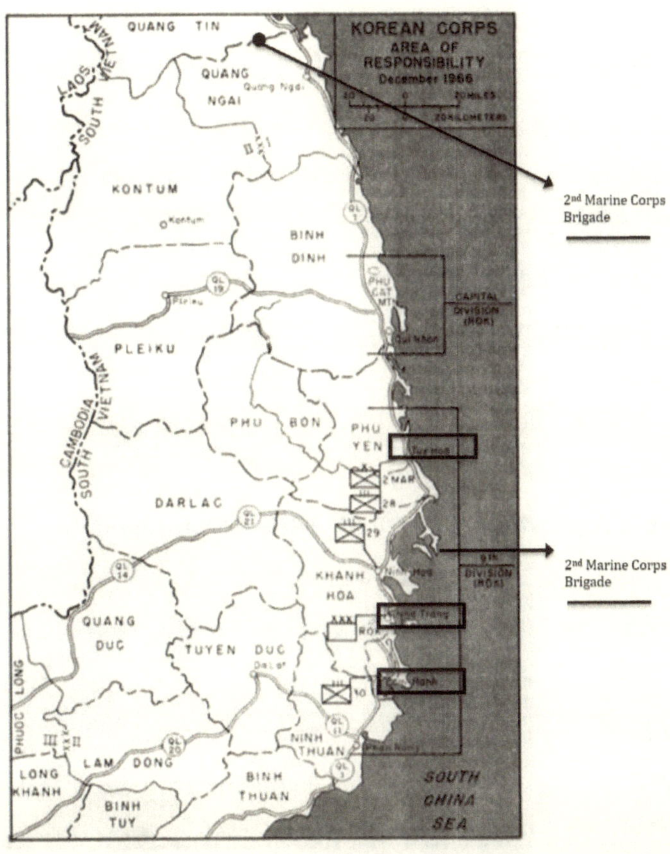

---

[102] Marek, Edward, "Koreans Rock-Solid in Vietnam." *Talking Proud.* (7 December 2013). <http://www.talkingproud.us/Military/ROKVIetnam/ROKVIetnamIntro.html>.

Operational Control of South Korean Military Forces

The US-Korean military relationship was unique among the agreements between the US and other Allied forces in Vietnam. American foreign policy publicized the Korean Army as an independent and administratively autonomous organization. The Johnson Administration felt that "…it would show… other countries that not only were the Koreans in a position to act on their own but they were also freely assisting the United States."[103] The truth, however, was far from what was broadcasted on American television.

The Verbal Agreement Between US-ROK Commanders

In January 1965, Major General Lee Sae Ho, Senior Korean officer in Vietnam, declared that his government would grant operation control of the inbound Dove Unit to American forces.[104] It was determined that the ROK would function under the Free World Military Policy Council. This meant that US General William C. Westmoreland possessed operational authority over non-combatant Korean troops, General Lee retained command of the ROK Dove Unit, and the Council would guide the upcoming Korean ground forces.[105]

On October 23rd, the Korean Divisions arrived in Vietnam.

---

[103] Larsen, Stanley R., and James Lawton Collins, *Allied Participation in Vietnam*, (Washington: Dept. of the Army: U.S. Govt). 1975. p.135

[104] Ibid. 123

[105] Ibid. 16, 133

That same day, Major General Chae Myung Shin, Commanding Officer of ROK forces, verbally assured General Westmoreland that "…whatever mission General Westmoreland gave him, he would execute it as if he were directly under Westmoreland's operational control."[106] Both men agreed that American directives to Korean units would be sent in the form of requests, but they would be honored as orders.[107]

(Commanding General of ROKF-V, Maj. Gen. Chae Myung Shin). [108]

A formal agreement was never signed between the US and Korea. General Westmoreland felt that an official arrangement could have been politically embarrassing for the Koreans as "…it might [have implied] that they were subordinate to, and acting as mercenaries for, the United States."[109] In the US General's opinion, a written agreement was

---

[106] Larsen, Stanley R., and James Lawton Collins, *Allied Participation in Vietnam*, (Washington: Dept. of the Army: U.S. Govt). 1975. p.133

[107] Ibid. 134

[108] Marek, Edward, "Koreans Rock-Solid in Vietnam." *Talking Proud.* (9 December 2013). <http://www.talkingproud.us/Military/ROKVIetnam/ROKVIetnamIntro.html>.

no longer necessary since General Chae had already granted de facto operational control by US commanders.[110] The bluntest incident to illustrate ROK combat troops as mercenary forces occurred when Korean President Park informed General Westmoreland that he was "…proud to have Koreans fighting under [his] command" during a visit to South Vietnam in 1966."[111] Figure 13. [112]

Capital "Tiger" Division

9th "White Horse" Division

2nd Marine "Blue Dragon" Brigade

---

[109] Ibid. 134

[110] Larsen, Stanley R., and James Lawton Collins, *Allied Participation in Vietnam*, (Washington: Dept. of the Army: U.S. Govt). 1975. p.134

[111] Ibid.146

[112] Marek, Edward, "Koreans Rock-Solid in Vietnam." *Talking Proud.* (9 December 2013). <http://www.talkingproud.us/Military/ROKVIetnam/ROKVIetnamIntro.html>.

4. CONSEQUENCES OF THE ROK'S INVOLVEMENT IN THE VIETNAM WAR

***

Domestic Ramifications (United States)

Foreign military involvement in South Vietnam ignited controversial political opposition throughout Congress. In 1967, US Senator Stephen R. Young investigated US-Korean negotiations. He compared the established arrangements to Great Britain's purchase of Hessian soldiers, who fought alongside the Redcoats during the Revolutionary War. Senator Young reminded Congress that a mercenary was defined as a person who served for pay in the armed forces of a foreign nation. He felt that Korea's agreement to receive American monetary funding switched their More Flags commitment from an assistance program to a mercenary operation.[113] As a result, Senator Young concluded that "…America was employing Korean mercenaries in South Vietnam."[114] The Johnson Administration responded by stating that Allied nations sending troops to Vietnam chose to do so "…of their own volition and for their own purposes…national interests and security, nothing more, nothing less."[115] However, of all the allied nations that sent soldiers to fight, Vietnam held no direct relevance to South Korea's national interests.[116]

---

[113] Blackburn, Robert M, *Mercenaries and Lyndon Johnson's "more Flags": The Hiring of Korean, Filipino, and Thai Soldiers in the Vietnam War*. Jefferson, NC: McFarland, 1994. p. 45

[114] Ibid. 66

[115] Ibid. 150

[116] One could argue that indirectly the Vietnamese conflict posed a national security threat for the ROK due to its potential influence for the removal of American forces from the 38th Parallel in order for them to fight in the Vietnam War. However, this claim is unfounded since major American troop withdrawals occurred nearly a decade before the ROK's involvement in SVN.

South Koreans on the Vietnamese Battlefield

(Korean soldiers encounter a tiger during stealth operations at the valley of Hon Ba Mountain – 1969) [117]

Domestic Ramifications (United States)

The Korean mission in Vietnam was to provide protection along the Eastern coast covering a radius of several hundred miles to prevent the renewal of NVA/VC harassment and domination.[118] The South Koreans requested to have their military forces deployed in an area where their presence could have the greatest impact at home and abroad. In essence, the ROK "…desired to put into play the military art the United States had taught them [in the Korean War] and prove that

[117] Jin-Hyun, Choi, "*[170] Slide Film - Vietnam War 1967*". *(englishp)*. (9 December 2013). <http://www.vietvet.co.kr/technote/read.cgi?board=englishp&x_number=1025350894&r_search=tiger&nnew=1>.

[118] Larsen, Stanley R., and James Lawton Collins, *Allied Participation in Vietnam*, (Washington: Dept. of the Army: U.S. Govt). 1975. p.145

their troops provided the man-to-man equivalent of American forces."[119]

(Figure 15) [120]

First, the ROK added a lethal and trustworthy dimension to Allied missions. While the Americans preferred to conduct large operations with heavy aerial support, the Korean forces favored small unit operations that focused on aggressive offensive raids, ambushes, and close-quarters hand-to-hand combat.[121] These tactics proved successful in joint US-Korean activities where targets hide in isolated areas. The ROK averaged 150 small unit actions per day, which included ambushes, search and destroy operations, and the normal efforts to secure areas.[122] Second, captured Viet Cong documents detailed the

---

[119] Ibid. 135

[120] Jin-Hyun, Choi, "*[170] Slide Film - Vietnam War 1967". (englishp).* (9 December 2013). <http://www.vietvet.co.kr/technote/read.cgi?board=englishp&x_number=1025350894&r_search=tiger&nnew=1>.

*The soldier pictured is An Sang-Byung (안상병). Battle of Dien Can – 27 November 1967.

[121] Marek, Edward, "Koreans Rock-Solid in Vietnam." *Talking Proud.* (9 December 2013). <http://www.talkingproud.us/Military/ROKVIetnam/ROKVIetnamIntro.html>.

[122] Larsen, Stanley R., and James Lawton Collins, *Allied Participation in Vietnam*, (Washington: Dept. of the Army: U.S. Govt). 1975. p.150

enemy's fear of the ROK. This sentiment was due to Korea's hardline view against Communism and its harsh treatment of enemy combatants. The VC worked hard to avoid the ROK and directed its activity mainly against American forces in civilian population centers. They only engaged Korean forces in open field when victory was certain, which rarely occurred.[123] Finally, the ROK were known for discovering numerous enemy weapons caches. They always conducted thorough searches during their operations and frequently had a higher weaponry count than American soldiers engaged in similar actions.[124]

(Figure 16) [125]

---

[123] Marek, Edward, "Koreans Rock-Solid in Vietnam." *Talking Proud.* (9 December 2013). <http://www.talkingproud.us/Military/ROKVIetnam/ROKVIetnamIntro.html>.
[124] Ibid. 143
[125] Ibid.

[The Code of Conduct of ROK Forces in Vietnam]

1. To the enemy, Be courageous and fearful.
2. To the Vietnamese people, Behave with kindness and warmness.
3. To our allies, show them we are well disciplined and reliable.

(Figure 17) [126]

ROK Corruption and Human Rights Violations

Illegal activity is synonymous with the word mercenary. Soldiers of fortune often operate without adequate regulation and proper mechanisms to ensure the accountability of their actions. The Koreans were closely tied to the emerging black market in Vietnam. It was reported that ROK forces were supplying off-post clubs and businesses with products bought from US military postal exchange (PX) outlets. In *The Village*, author Bing West commented on these alleged activities. He wrote,

"In the town of Bihn Son PX goods, liquor, narcotics, medicinal supplies, American cigarettes, silk, and prostitutes were being sold. The Americans could not take action because Binh Son was in a Korean sector, and the Vietnamese officials did not want to act because they were getting rich."[127]

---

[126] Jin-Hyun, Choi, "*[170] Slide Film - Vietnam War 1967*". *(englishp)*. (9 December 2013). <http://www.vietvet.co.kr/technote/read.cgi?board=englishp&x_number=1025350894&r_search=tig er&nnew=1>.

[127] West, Francis, *The village*. New York, NY: Pocket Books, 2003. p. 326

*Senior American commanders removed the Korean commander of Bihn Son shortly after it was found out that he had called a hit on a junior US Lieutenant meddling in the town's black marketing operations.

ROK forces were also known for their authoritative treatment of Vietnamese locals. When conducting military operations, Korean soldiers remained in an area to interrogate villagers until they believed all information had been exploited.[128] For example, Korean military forces near the Muy Ba Mountain made life so difficult for local villagers that the entire population gradually moved out of the area.[129] Harry McPherson, a special counsel to the US president, concluded that the ROK "…had 'created as many problems as they [had] solved…they are too brutal and careless of civilian life.'"[130]

(ROK Marine escorting three Viet Cong prisoners to be interrogated near Tuy Hoa – 1966) [131]

---

[128] Larsen, Stanley R., and James Lawton Collins, *Allied Participation in Vietnam*, (Washington: Dept. of the Army: U.S. Govt). 1975. p.155

[129] Ibid. 135

[130] Colman, J. and Widen, J. J. (2009), The Johnson Administration and the Recruitment of Allies in Vietnam, 1964–1968. (2 December 2013). p. 500
<http://onlinelibrary.wiley.com/doi/10.1111/j.1468-229X.2009.00467.x/full>.

[131] Marek, Edward, "Koreans Rock-Solid in Vietnam." *Talking Proud.* (9 December 2013). <http://www.talkingproud.us/Military/ROKVIetnam/ROKVIetnamIntro.html>.

54

CONCLUSION

***

Mercenaries in the Vietnam War has presented an argument that illustrates the Republic of Korea's presence in South Vietnam as a mercenary force hired by the United States. After discussing the context and overview of the Vietnam War and defining the term mercenary, this book analyzed the reasons behind South Korea's desire to participate in the conflict: 1) America's military involvement in the Korean Peninsula. 2) Korean President Park Chung Hee and his model for economic development. 3) Legacy of the Vietnam War on the Korean economy.

The following chapters presented four factors challenging the conventional wisdom of South Korea's involvement in the conflict: 1) President Lyndon B. Johnson's "More Flags" program. 2) Detailing why the other Allied forces participating in the war were not classified as "mercenaries." 3) Washington's complete financial support of the ROK's involvement in Vietnam. 4) The verbal agreement established by US-ROK commanders regarding operational control of South Korean military forces. Through an analysis of each of these factors by examining the logic and evidence of all explanations, this literary work concluded that a synthesis of American financial assistance and secret agreements made between the US and ROK over operational control were the most compelling factors to classify the ROK's army as a mercenary force in service to America.

Mercenaries in the Vietnam War continued by examining the implications of the ROK's deployment of troops to South Vietnam, concluding that the Johnson Administration utilized their presence in Vietnam as a way to silence growing domestic opposition to the conflict. Additionally, it examined Korea's overall performance in the conflict confirming that the ROK's military provided a man-to-man equivalent of American forces. In the final chapter, this book displayed two consequences (corruption and human rights violations) synonymous with mercenary forces fighting an elusive enemy in unfamiliar territory.

BIBLIOGRAPHY

✻✻✻

Baek, Glen. "A Perspective on Korea's Participation in the Vietnam
War." *The Asan Institute for Policy Studies* 53 (2013): 1-10. Print.

Blackburn, Robert M. *Mercenaries and Lyndon Johnson's "more Flags": The
Hiring of Korean, Filipino, and Thai Soldiers in the Vietnam War.*
Jefferson, NC: McFarland, 1994. Print.

Castle, Timothy N. *At war in the shadow of Vietnam: U.S. military aid to the
Royal Lao government, 1955-1975.* New York: Columbia University
Press, 1993. Print.

Colman, J. and Widen, J. (2009), The Johnson Administration and the
Recruitment of Allies in Vietnam, 1964–1968. History, 94: 483–
504. Web. 18 Apr. 2012.
<http://onlinelibrary.wiley.com/doi/10.1111/j.1468-
229X.2009.00467.x/full>.

"Digital History." *Digital History.* N.p., n.d. Web. 5 Dec. 2013.
<http://www.digitalhistory.uh.edu/era.cfm?eraid=18&smtid=
1>.

Foreign Relations of the United States, 1961-1963 XXII (1961): 1-10. Print.

Gaines, Kyle. *The Decisive Factors in the UN Forces' Defense of the Pusan
Perimeter in the 1950 Korean War,* (Potomac Foundation): 3-5.
Print.

"Geneva Conventions." *Wikipedia.* N.p., n.d. Web. 20 Dec. 1992.
<http://en.wikipedia.org/wiki/File:Original_Geneva_Convent
ions.jpg>.

Hickman, Kennedy. "Vietnam 101: A Short Introduction." *About.com
Military History.* N.p., n.d. Web. 6 Dec. 2013.
<http://militaryhistory.about.com/od/vietnamwar/p/Vietna
mBrief.htm>.

Jin-Hyun, Choi. "*[170] Slide Film - Vietnam War 1967." (englishp).* N.p.,
n.d. Web. 10 Dec. 2013.
<http://www.vietvet.co.kr/technote/read.cgi?board=englishp

&x_number=1025350894&r_search=tiger&nnew=1>.

Kim, Hyung. *Korea's development under Park Chung Hee rapid industrialization, 1961-79.* London: RoutledgeCurzon, 2004. Print.

"Korea - GDP per capita." *Index Mundi.* N.p., n.d. Web. 5 May 2014. <http://www.indexmundi.com/facts/korea/gdp-per-capita>.

"Korean Veterans of the Vietnam War." *ROK Home.* Web. 03 Apr. 2012. <http://mcel.pacificu.edu/as/students/koreavet/home.htm>.

Larsen, Stanley R., and James Lawton Collins. *Allied Participation in Vietnam.* Washington: Dept. of the Army: for Sale by the Supt. of Docs., U.S. Govt. Print. Off., 1975. Print.

Lee, Min Y. "The Vietnam War: South Korea's Search for National Security." *International Relations.* 403-29. Web. 18 Apr. 2012. <https://campus.georgetown.edu/bbcswebdav/pid-2443148-dt-content-rid-2105902_1/courses/HIST-226-01.Spring2012/DOC001-4%281%29.PDF>.

Marek, Edward. "Koreans Rock-Solid in Vietnam." *Talking Proud.* Web. 18 Apr. 2012. <http://www.talkingproud.us/Military/ROKVIetnam/ROKVI etnamIntro.html>.

"May 16 coup." *Wikipedia.* Wikimedia Foundation, 5 Aug. 2014. Web. 8 May 2014. <http://en.wikipedia.org/wiki/May_16_coup>.

"Meeting with General Chung Hee Park, Chairman, Supreme Council of Korea, 3:30PM." - *John F. Kennedy Presidential Library & Museum.* N.p., n.d. Web. 8 May 2014. <http://www.jfklibrary.org/Asset-Viewer/Archives/JFKWHP-1961-11-14-C.aspx>.

"Mercenary." *Merriam-Webster.* Merriam-Webster, n.d. Web. 8 Dec. 2013. <http://www.merriam-webster.com/dictionary/mercenary>.

"Park Chung-Hee and the Economy of South Korea." N.p., n.d. (0): 1-17. Print.

Park, Chung Hee. *Korea Reborn: A Model for Development*. Englewood Cliffs, N.J.: Prentice-Hall, 1979. Print.

Pemberton, Gregory. *All the way: Australia's road to Vietnam*. Sydney: Allen & Unwin, 1987. Print.

"Primary source: "Myth vs. Reality" by B.G. Burkett and GlennaWhitley." *Vietnam (RVN) War Chronology/Timeline*. N.p., n.d. Web. 7 Dec. 2013. <http://cybersarges.tripod.com/timeline.html>.

Rabel, Roberto Giorgio. *New Zealand and the Vietnam war: politics and diplomacy*. Auckland, N.Z.: Auckland University Press, 2005. Print

"ROK Drop Review: Bing West's, The Village | ROK Drop." *ROK Drop RSS*. N.p., n.d. Web. 6 Dec. 2013. <http://rokdrop.com/2008/06/04/rok-drop-review-bing-wests-the-village/>.

Scalapino, Robert A.. *Korea-U.S. relations: the politics of trade and security*. Berkeley: Institute of East Asian Studies, University of California, 1988. Print.

Scott, Peter. *Lost crusade: America's secret Cambodian mercenaries*. Annapolis, Md.: Naval Institute Press, 1998. Print.

"Secrets behind Korea's Economic Success." *YouTube*. The Korea Foundation, 12 Dec. 2013. Web. 5 May 2014. <https://www.youtube.com/watch?v=bJ0hMr5TSkI>.

Shadow company. Dir. Nick Bicanic . Perf. Alan Bell, Phil Lancaster. Purpose Built Film, 2006. Film.

Shultz, Richard H.. *The secret war against Hanoi: Kennedy's and Johnson's use of spies, saboteurs, and covert warriors in North Vietnam*. New York: HarperCollins, 1999. Print.

Sneider, Richard L.. *The political and social capabilities of North and South Korea for the long-term military competition*. Santa Monica, CA: Rand, 1985. Print.

"U.S. paid S.Korean victims of Vietnam War." *UPI*. N.p., 2 Dec. 2005.
    Web. 5 May 2014.
        <http://www.upi.com/Top_News/2005/12/02/US-paid-
        SKorean-victims-of-Vietnam-War/UPI-80431133524267/>.

Vietnam in HD. Dir. Michael Hall. Perf. Adrian Grenier . A & E Home
    Video, 2011. Blu-Ray.

Walzer, Michael. *Just and unjust wars: a moral argument with historical
    illustrations*. 4th ed. New York: Basic Books, 20061977. Print.

West, Francis. *The village*. New York, NY: Pocket Books, 2003. Print.

Westmoreland, William C.. *A soldier reports*. Garden City, N.Y.:
    Doubleday, 1976. Print.

Won-soon, Park. "Korea-Japan Treaty, Breakthrough for Nation
    Building." *The Korea Times*. N.p., 19 Mar. 2010. Web. 5 May
    2014.
    <http://www.koreatimes.co.kr/www/news/biz/2013/11/291_
    62653.html>.

ACKNOWLEDGMENT

***

Mercenaries in the Vietnam War has been over a year-long adventure. I would like to acknowledge the following people, without whose cooperation and assistance this project would not have been possible: Ms. Christine Kim, Georgetown University Interim Director of Studies – Asian Studies Program (ASP), who encouraged and recognized the value of this story; Mr. Scott LaFoy for providing translated and confidential manuscripts of the communications between President Park Chung Hee, President John F. Kennedy, and President Lyndon B. Johnson; Professor Phillip Karber, President of the Potomac Foundation, who reviewed an abundance of content over several months. Finally, I dedicate this book to the soldiers who served and made the ultimate sacrifice in the Vietnam War for it is not the war I know, it is the war they fought.

The study of Korea's participation in the Vietnam War is highly time-consuming due to the relative dearth of scholarship and writing on the subject. Despite this scarcity, my research has yet to cover all areas of the topic. For the next volume of *Mercenaries in the Vietnam War*, I intend to examine the contemporary portrayal of South Korean involvement in the conflict within mainstream Korean literature and cinema. Additionally, I plan to expand my investigation on allegations of ROK corruption and Human Rights violations. Finally, I would like to conduct a poll targeted specifically at Korean college students in the Washington, D.C. area (Georgetown University, George Washington University, and American University). The survey would analyze if young Korean adults studying in the United States are keenly aware of their country's involvement in the Vietnam War, the economic benefits it brought on Korean society, and other relative questions regarding the topic. The results would shed light on contemporary Korean student views of their country's participation in the war.

ABOUT THE AUTHOR

Charles Martin Hernández-Hermann graduated from St. John's Northwestern Military Academy as class valedictorian in 2011. He continued his academic studies at Georgetown University's School of Foreign Service majoring in International Politics and Security Studies. Raised in Guanajuato, México, Charles speaks fluent Spanish and holds a keen interest in Turkish and Mandarin Chinese.

Captain (CPT) Charles Hernández is currently an active-duty Army officer serving in the 3rd US Infantry Regiment, The Old Guard – Official Escort to the President of the United States. His military accolades include the Ranger Tab, Parachutist Badge, and Expert Infantryman Badge. CPT Hernández previously campaigned closely with NATO Allies and Partner Nations in eight countries and four multinational military exercises of Operation Atlantic Resolve.

www.ingramcontent.com/pod-product-compliance
Lightning Source LLC
Chambersburg PA
CBHW051226250726
48655CB00006B/2623